*e*MoviePoster*.com*

presents

Vintage Hollywood Posters VI

Every item pictured in this book will be auctioned by **eMoviePoster.com** on the Internet from 12/09/03–12/16/03 (all items will close on 12/16/03 between 7 PM CST & 10 PM CST). Complete detailed descriptions of every item (including high quality digital images and detailed condition descriptions) can be found on our website **http://www.emovieposter.com**

IN THIS AUCTION THERE ARE:
NO Buyer's Premiums
NO U.S. Shipping Charges
NO Sales Taxes (except in Missouri)
See our website for full details!

Edited and Published by Bruce Hershenson
P.O. Box 874, West Plains, MO 65775
Phone: **(417) 256-9616** Fax: **(417) 257-6948**
mail@brucehershenson.com (e-mail)
http://**www.emovieposter.com** (website)

INTRODUCTION

My name is Bruce Hershenson and in 1990 I organized the very first all-movie poster auction ever held by a major auction house! It was a complete success, with all 271 lots selling for just under one million dollars. Since then I organized 12 more major "live" movie poster auctions (nine more for Christie's auction house and three for Howard Lowery auctions) with total sales of just under ten million dollars. In between, I sold over 30,000 movie posters and lobby cards through semi-annual sales catalogs with sales of over four million dollars.

In 1999 I opened eMoviePoster.com on the Internet, which has since become the most visited vintage movie poster website, with nearly 600,000 visitors to date. In mid-2000 I started weekly Tuesday night auctions on the eBay auction site, and in over 175 nearly consecutive weekly auctions to date have auctioned more than 100,000 items on eBay, with total sales of just under SIX million dollars!

I published an elaborate full-color auction catalog for each major auction I organized (just like what you are holding in your hands), and in addition have published 21 reference volumes to movie posters, for a total of 36 volumes to date, which combined have sold more than 270,000 copies!

In 2001 I decided to move my major auctions to the Internet. On June 30 and July 1, 2001 (in Vintage Hollywood Posters IV), I auctioned 711 items for a total of $717,000. Those who have purchased items at other major auctions are all too familiar with the many added fees tacked on after the auction's close, including a buyer's premium that ranges from 15% to 20%, and shipping fees that range from high to outrageous. But in Vintage Hollywood Posters IV, there were NO Buyer's Premiums, NO U.S. Shipping charges, and NO Sales Tax (except in Missouri). This saved most buyers from 30% to 40% compared to purchasing at other major auctions!

I also provided complete detailed descriptions of every item. Many major auctions only provide bidders with fuzzy images and fuzzier condition descriptions, glossing over condition defects and restoration. I provided high quality digital images, and detailed condition descriptions (including detailed descriptions of each restored item's PRE-restoration condition, something NO other major auction house provides).

In 2002 I repeated the process with Vintage Hollywood Posters V. The 385 items in this auction were auctioned on December 14, 2002, for a total of $518,000+ (the top lot sold for $67,000+).

NOW I PRESENT MY THIRD MAJOR ONLINE AUCTION, VINTAGE HOLLYWOOD POSTERS VI. The auction ends on 12-16-03 (there will be preliminary bidding from December 9th to 16th).

ONCE AGAIN, THERE ARE NO BUYER'S PREMIUMS, NO U.S. SHIPPING CHARGES AND NO SALES TAX (except in Missouri), which will again save buyers 30% to 40%! Also, note that in Vintage Hollywood Posters VI, you will find many items that are financially well within the reach of ANY collector. But I did not sacrifice quality to include these more reasonably priced items. I carefully sought out the most desired lobby cards and posters from the best films of the past 50 years, the kind of items that most collectors are actively seeking, but have great difficulty finding, especially in top condition.

AN IMPORTANT ANNOUNCEMENT REGARDING THE POSTERS AND LOBBY CARDS IN THIS VOLUME!

Unless otherwise noted, EVERY image is of the FIRST U.S. release one-sheet movie poster. All of the items pictured in this book will be auctioned by eMoviePoster.com on the Internet on 12/16/03. If you are reading this PRIOR to that date, go to http://www.emovieposter.com to find out how to bid (if you don't have Internet access, call (417) 256-9616 and we'll make arrangements for you to bid another way). If you are reading this AFTER 12/16/03, you will find a sheet added to this volume that gives the prices every item sold for. If you have items you would like us to consider for our future auctions, go to http://www.emovieposter.com/consign.htm and read our terms, or, if you don't have Internet access, call us or mail us a list of your posters (see the first page of this book for full contact info). If you are interested in buying movie posters or lobby cards, or in learning more about the hobby, you should visit our website at http://www.emovieposter.com, where you will find thousands of images of the very best movie posters, as well as lots of information important to every collector. You can find out all you need to know about bidding on items in this most exciting auction (larger images, detailed condition descriptions, etc.) by going to my website, http://www.emovieposter.com

---

Phillip Wages (who created the online auctions and much of my website), David Graveen (who did much of the photography), and Amy Knight (who did the layouts and cover design for this books and many of my previous books) gave considerable assistance in the preparation of this auction and this catalog, and I thank them very much. I also must thank my wonderful wife, Sylvia Hershenson, who gave me much needed support during the preparation of this auction!

Bruce Hershenson

November, 2003

1. VERTIGO, 1958

2. VERTIGO, 1958, Style A half-sheet

3. VERTIGO, 1958, Style B half-sheet

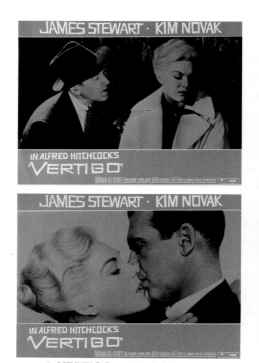

4. VERTIGO, 1958, lobby cards

5. REAR WINDOW, 1954, half-sheet

6. REBECCA, 1940, Australian daybill

7. TO CATCH A THIEF, 1955, half-sheet

8. NORTH BY NORTHWEST, 1959, half-sheet

9. SPELLBOUND, 1945, half-sheet

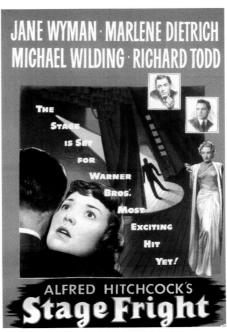

10. STAGE FRIGHT, 1950

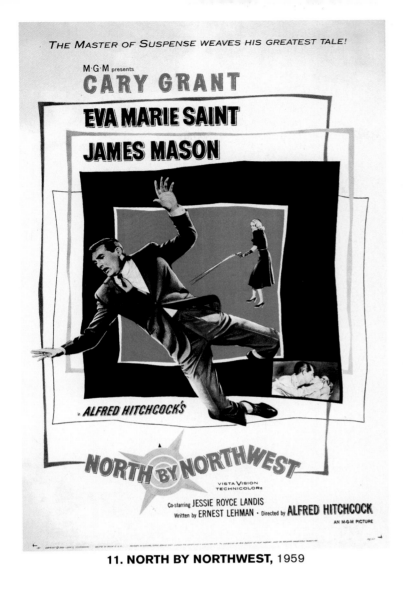

11. NORTH BY NORTHWEST, 1959

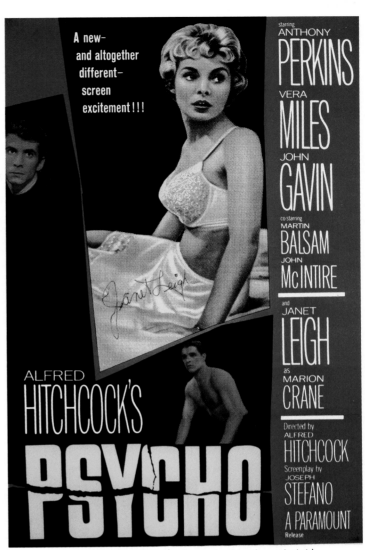

12. PSYCHO, 1960, (autographed by Janet Leigh)

13. SHADOW OF A DOUBT, 1943, half-sheet

14. FOREIGN CORRESPONDENT. 1940,
Italian one-sheet

15. PLANET OF THE APES, 1968

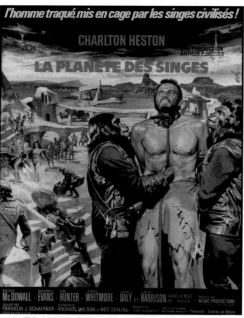

16. PLANET OF THE APES, 1968, French

17. MUNSTER, GO HOME, 1966

18. GO APE, 1974

19. GO APE, 1974, (TV style)

20. MUNSTER, GO HOME, 1966, three-sheet

21. THX 1138, 1970, British quad

22. THX 1138, 1970

23. HAUNTED GOLD, 1932

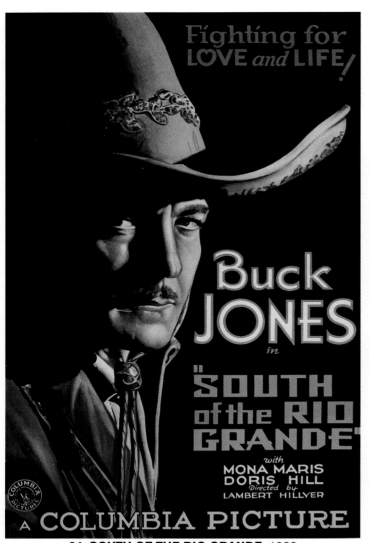

24. SOUTH OF THE RIO GRANDE, 1932

25. STAGECOACH, 1939, jumbo window card

26. RIO BRAVO, 1959, three-sheet

27. STAGECOACH, 1939, lobby card (autographed by John Wayne & Andy Devine)

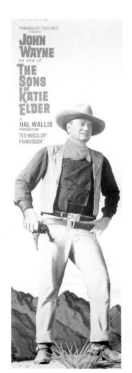

28. THE SONS OF KATIE ELDER, 1965, 4 door panels

29. THE ALAMO, 1960

30. DAVY CROCKETT, KING OF THE WILD FRONTIER,
1955, Forty By Sixty

31. THE OUTLAW, 1943,
Australian daybill, circa 1946 release

32. THE OUTLAW, 1943,
Australian daybill, circa 1949 release

33. JAILHOUSE ROCK, 1957

34. LOVE ME TENDER, 1956, insert

35. BLUE HAWAII, 1961

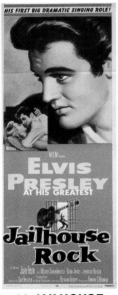

36. JAILHOUSE ROCK, 1957, insert

37. JAILHOUSE ROCK, 1957, French

38. JAILHOUSE ROCK, 1957, Swedish

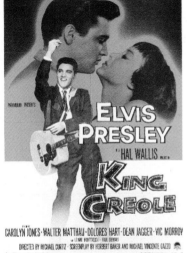

39. KING CREOLE, 1958

40. VIVA LAS VEGAS, 1964

41. LOVING YOU, 1957

42. THE WAR OF THE WORLDS, 1953, six-sheet

43. NOT OF THIS EARTH, 1957, three-sheet

44. THE MONOLITH MONSTERS, 1957, six-sheet

45. CONQUEST OF SPACE, 1955, six-sheet

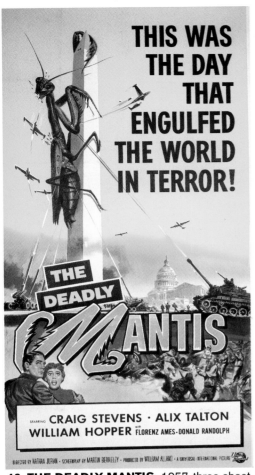

46. THE DEADLY MANTIS, 1957, three-sheet

47. INVADERS FROM MARS, 1953, six-sheet

48. THE DEADLY MANTIS, 1957

49. THE SHE-CREATURE, 1956

50. THE FLY, 1958

51. WHEN WORLDS COLLIDE, 1951, Italian

52. QUEEN OF OUTER SPACE, 1958

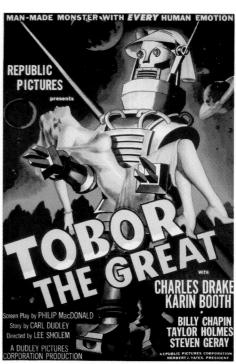

53. TOBOR THE GREAT, 1954

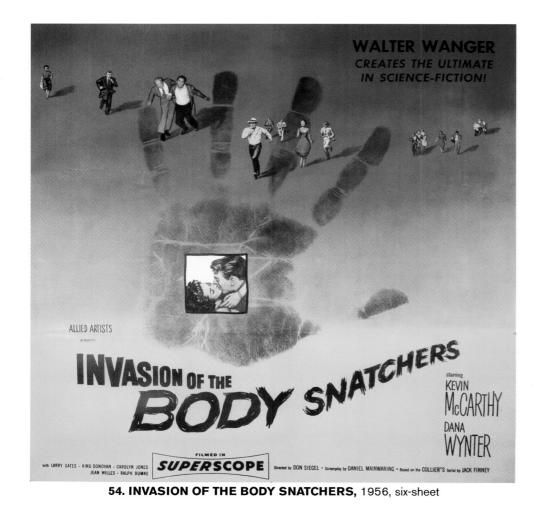

54. INVASION OF THE BODY SNATCHERS, 1956, six-sheet

55. REPTILICUS, 1962, three-sheet

56. THE LAND UNKNOWN, 1957, six-sheet

57. COMMANDO CODY, 1953

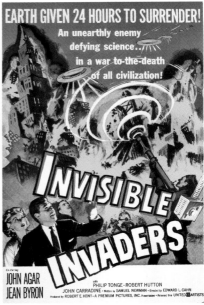

58. INVISIBLE INVADERS, 1959

59. HOUSE ON HAUNTED HILL, 1959,
three-sheet

60. THE INCREDIBLE SHRINKING MAN, 1957, six-sheet

61. REVENGE OF THE CREATURE, 1955, six-sheet

62. BEAST FROM HAUNTED CAVE,
1959, three-sheet

63. THE GHOUL, 1933, lobby card

64. THE BRIDE OF FRANKENSTEIN, 1935, local theater jumbo window card

65. KING KONG, 1933, Swedish, 1938 re-release

66. FRANKENSTEIN, 1931, herald

67. FRANKENSTEIN, 1931, German program

68. THE OLD DARK HOUSE, 1932, herald

69. WHITE ZOMBIE, 1932, herald

70. BRIDE OF THE MONSTER,
1956, Forty By Sixty

71. MAD LOVE, 1935, window card

72. MARK OF THE VAMPIRE, 1935, window card

73. THE DEATH KISS, 1932

74. SNOW WHITE AND THE SEVEN DWARFS, 1938, title card
75.-81 SNOW WHITE AND THE SEVEN DWARFS, 1938, lobby cards

82. ALICE GETS IN DUTCH, 1924

83. SNOW WHITE AND THE SEVEN DWARFS, 1938, Czech insert

84. LET'S STICK TOGETHER, 1952

85. WALT DISNEY STARS, 1947

86. VICTORY THROUGH AIR POWER, 1943, lobby cards

87. PETER PAN, 1953

88. SO DEAR TO MY HEART, 1949

89. SONG OF THE SOUTH, 1946

90. FUN AND FANCY FREE, 1947

91. ONE HUNDRED AND ONE DALMATIANS, 1961

92. T-BONE HANDICAP, c.1932

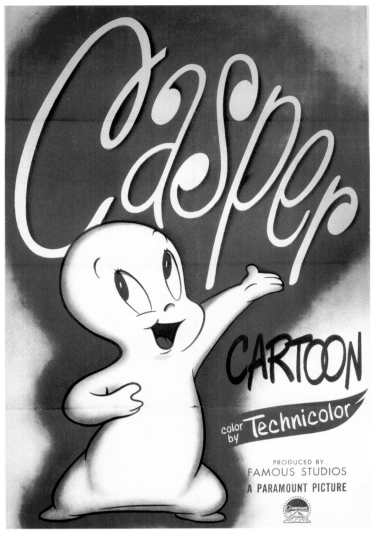

93. CASPER, 1950

94. POPEYE THE SAILOR MAN, 1934, Swedish

95. GULLIVER'S TRAVELS, 1939, Swedish

96. CITIZEN KANE, 1940

97. THE MAGNIFICENT AMBERSONS, 1942, half-sheet

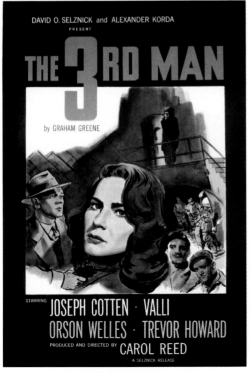

98. THE 3RD MAN, 1949

99. THE 3RD MAN, 1949, lobby card

100. THE BLUE DAHLIA, 1946

101. OUT OF THE PAST, 1947, Australian one-sheet

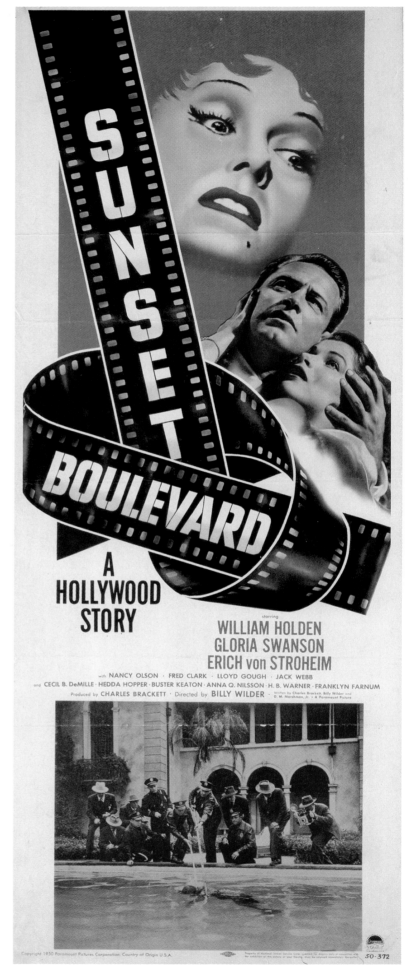

102. SUNSET BLVD, 1950, insert

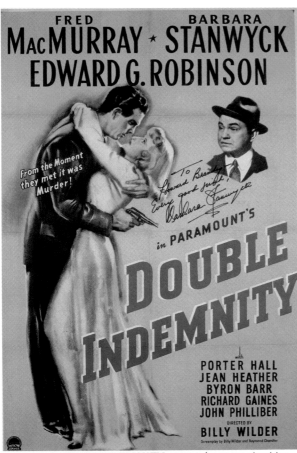

103. DOUBLE INDEMNITY, 1944 (autographed by Barbara Stanwyck)

104. LAURA, 1944, Australian daybill

105. DARK PASSAGE, 1947, Australian daybill

106. LAURA, 1944, half-sheet

107. DARK PASSAGE, 1947, French

108. GILDA, 1946, Argentinean

109. AFFAIR IN TRINIDAD, 1952

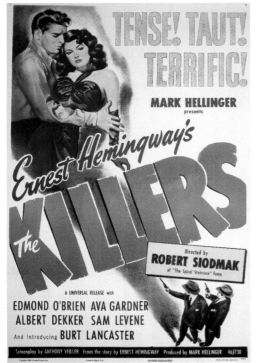

110. THE KILLERS, 1946

111. I WALK ALONE, 1948

112. PITFALL, 1948

113. IMPACT, 1949

114. CORNERED, 1946

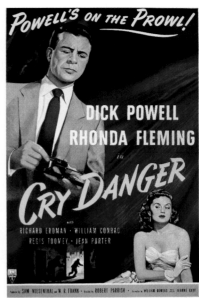

115. CRY DANGER, 1951

116. THE DARK PAST, 1949

117. JOHNNY O'CLOCK, 1946

118. BUNCO SQUAD, 1950

119. WHERE THE SIDEWALK ENDS, 1950

120. CRACK-UP, 1946

121. ROADBLOCK, 1951

122. PHANTOM LADY, 1944

123. JUKE GIRL, 1942,
Australian daybill

124. I LOVE TROUBLE, 1947

125. SO EVIL MY LOVE, 1948

126. MAN BAIT, 1952

127. WILD FOR KICKS, 1965

128. BEAUTY AND THE BEAST, 1946, French

129. NAPOLEON, 1927, French, 1930's re-release

130. ANDREI RUBLEV, 1969, Russian

131. LOS OLVIDADOS, 1950, Mexican

132. 1000 EYES OF DR. MABUSE, 1966, German

133. OPEN CITY, 1946, Italian one-sheet

134. THE BICYCLE THIEF, 1948, Italian

135. THE BICYCLE THIEF, 1948,
Italian photobustas

136. THE BICYCLE THIEF,
1948, Italian locandina

137. MIRACLE OF MILAN, 1951,
Italian portfolio (autographed by De Sica)

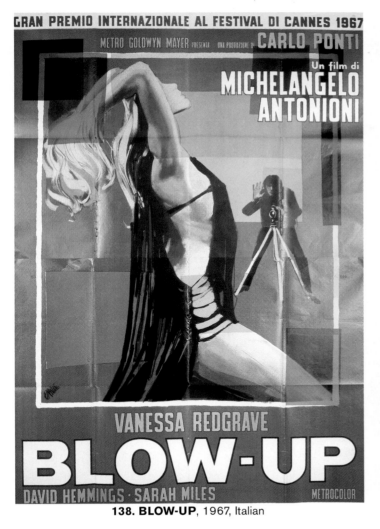

138. BLOW-UP, 1967, Italian

139. THE THREE TREASURES, 1959, Japanese

141. PICKPOCKET, 1959, French

142. LA DOLCE VITA, 1961,
Italian locandina

143. THE 400 BLOWS, 1959, French

140. RAN, 1985, Japanese

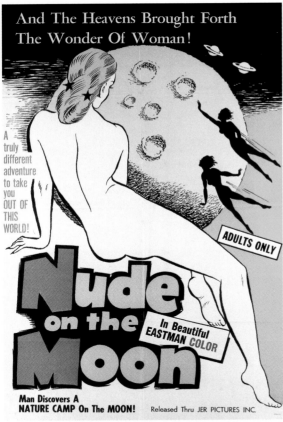

144. **NUDE ON THE MOON**, 1962

145. **THE AMAZON HEAD HUNTERS**, 1931

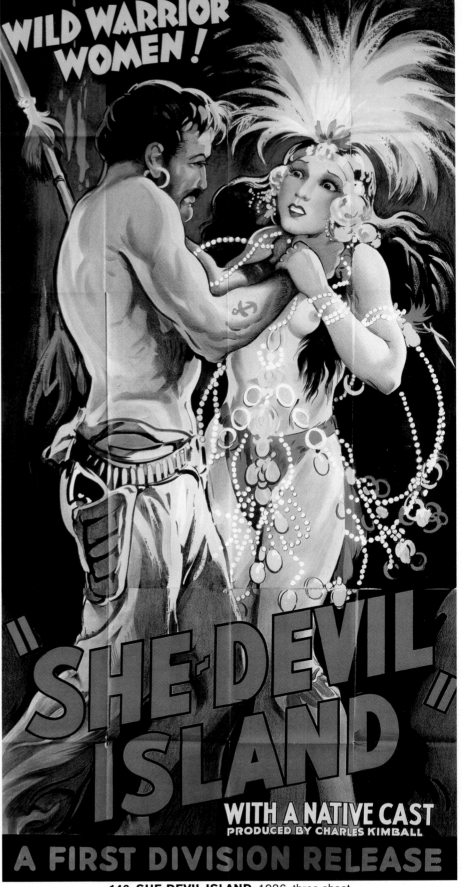

146. **SHE-DEVIL ISLAND**, 1936, three-sheet

147. NETTING THE LEOPARD, c.1922

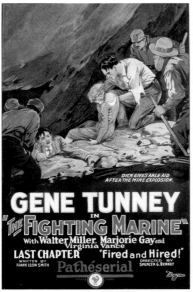

148. THE FIGHTING MARINE, 1926

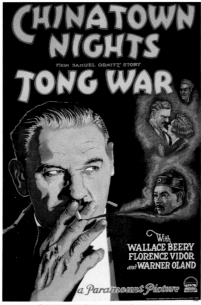

149. CHINATOWN NIGHTS, 1929

150. THE BIG PARADE, 1925, three-sheet

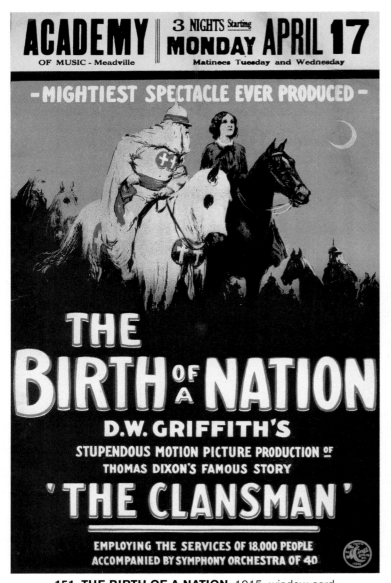

151. THE BIRTH OF A NATION, 1915, window card

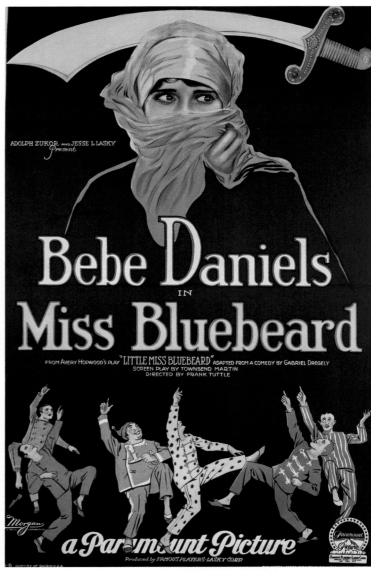

152. MISS BLUEBEARD, 1925

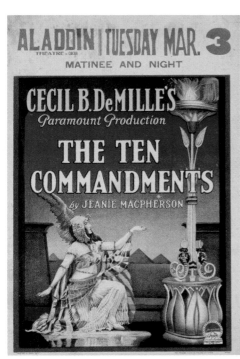

153. THE TEN COMMANDMENTS,
1923, window card

**154. MACISTE AGAINST THE
KIDNAPPERS**, c.1925

155. LOVES OF CASANOVA, 1927

156. TAMILLA, c.1935, Russian

157. THROUGH THE BREAKERS, 1928

158. FORBIDDEN LOVE, 1927

159. CHANG, 1927, Australian daybill

160. OLD IRONSIDES, 1926, Australian daybill

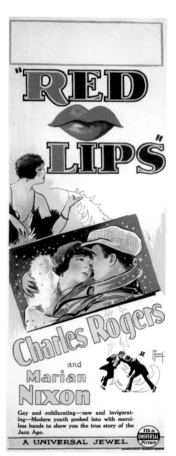

161. RED LIPS, 1928, Australian daybill

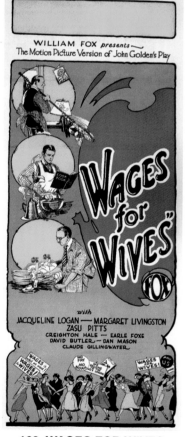

162. WAGES FOR WIVES, 1925, Australian daybill

163. THE WEREWOLF OF LONDON, 1935

164. KING KONG, 1933, Czech

165. THE GHOST OF FRANKENSTEIN, 1942, half-sheet, circa 1949 re-release

167. THE MUMMY'S CURSE, 1944, lobby card

168. THE MUMMY'S GHOST, 1944, French

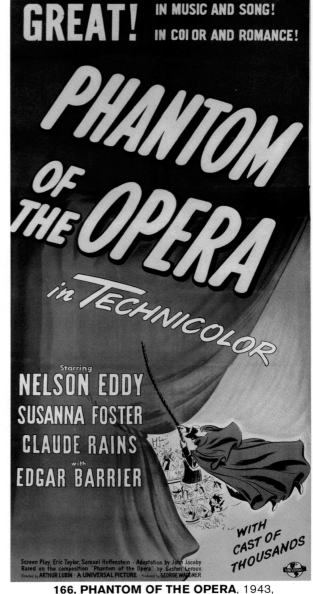

166. PHANTOM OF THE OPERA, 1943, three-sheet

169. ISLE OF THE DEAD, 1945

170. MIGHTY JOE YOUNG, 1949, 1953 re-release

171. THE SON OF DR. JEKYLL, 1951, six-sheet

172. FORBIDDEN PLANET, 1956, half-sheet

173. GODZILLA, 1956

174. INVADERS FROM MARS, 1953

175. FORBIDDEN PLANET, 1956, title card **176-182. FORBIDDEN PLANET**, 1956, lobby cards

183. CREATURE FROM THE BLACK LAGOON, 1954, half-sheet

184. REVENGE OF THE CREATURE, 1955

185. THE CREATURE WALKS AMONG US, 1956, window card

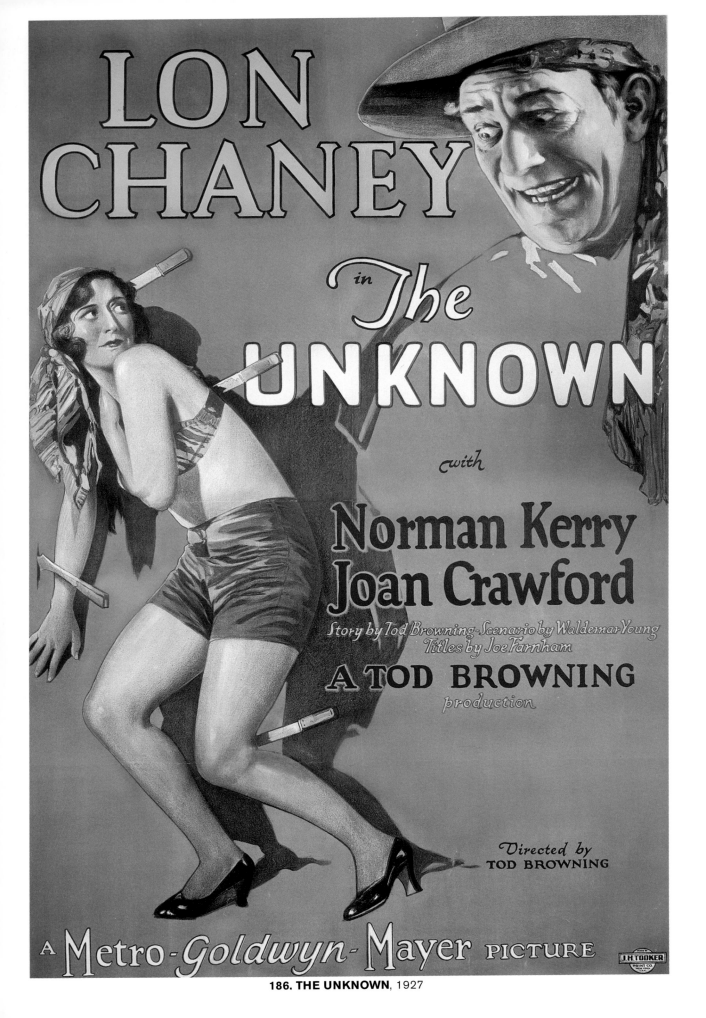

186. THE UNKNOWN, 1927

187. SHADOWS, 1961, window card

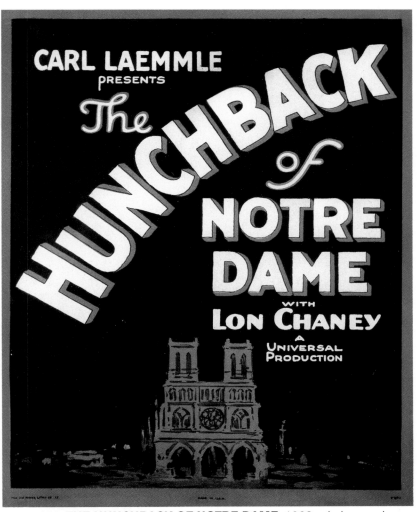

188. THE HUNCHBACK OF NOTRE DAME, 1923, window card

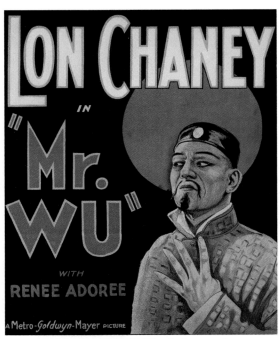

189. MR. WU, 1927, window card

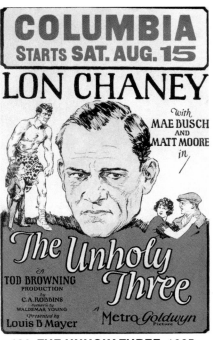

190. THE UNHOLY THREE, 1925, window card

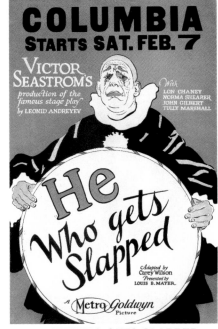

191. HE WHO GETS SLAPPED, 1924, window card

192. THE SEVEN YEAR ITCH, 1955

193. THE SEVEN YEAR ITCH, 1955, title card

194. SOME LIKE IT HOT, 1959, three-sheet

195. THE PRINCE AND THE SHOWGIRL, 1957, six-sheet

196. GENTLEMEN PREFER BLONDES,
1953, three-sheet

197. GENTLEMEN PREFER BLONDES, 1953

**198. GENTLEMEN
PREFER BLONDES,** 1953,
lobby cards

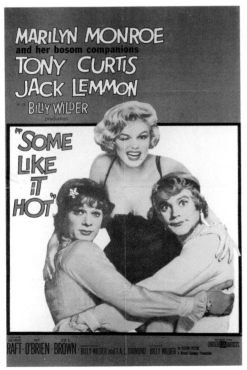

199. SOME LIKE IT HOT, 1959

200. LADIES OF THE CHORUS, 1948, lobby card

201. DOUGH BOYS, 1930

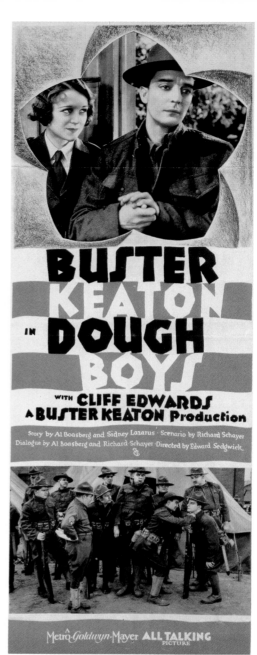

202. DOUGH BOYS, 1930, insert

203. AN OLD SPANISH CUSTOM, 1935

204. ONE A.M., 1917,
c. 1932 re-release

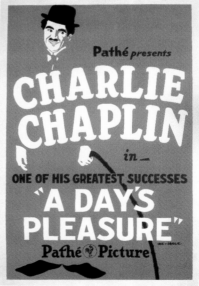

205. A DAY'S PLEASURE, 1919,
c. 1924 re-release

206. THE LADY EVE, 1941

207. ROOM SERVICE, 1938, window card

208. A DAY AT THE RACES, 1937, insert

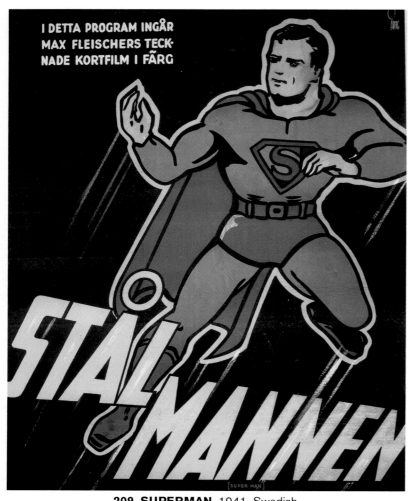

209. SUPERMAN, 1941, Swedish

210. SUPERMAN, 1948

211. SUPERMAN IN EXILE, 1954

212. DARKEST AFRICA, 1936

213. THE SHADOW RETURNS, 1946

214. SUPERMAN, 1978, British quad

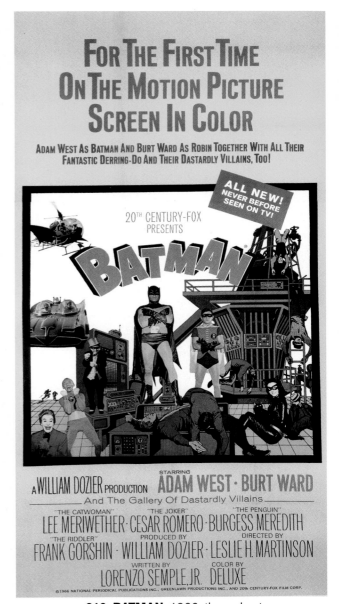

216. BATMAN, 1966, three-sheet

215. SUPERMAN, 1978, British quad

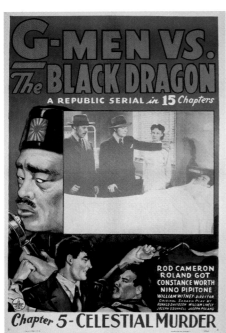

217. G-MEN VS. THE BLACK DRAGON, 1943

218. THE GREEN HORNET STRIKES AGAIN, 1940

219. BATMAN, 1966, French

220. APOCALYPSE NOW, 1979, German

221. APOCALYPSE NOW, 1979, Japanese

222. THE ENDLESS SUMMER, 1967, special poster

223. THE ENDLESS SUMMER, 1967, British quad

226. HAROLD AND MAUDE, 1971, English

225. WALKABOUT, 1971, Australian daybill

224. DELIVERANCE, 1972, six-sheet

227. PAINTED POST, 1928

228. THE GREAT K AND A TRAIN ROBBERY, 1926

229. MY OWN PAL, 1926

230. THE LAST TRAIL, 1927

231. TUMBLING RIVER, 1927

232. THE DRIFTER, 1929

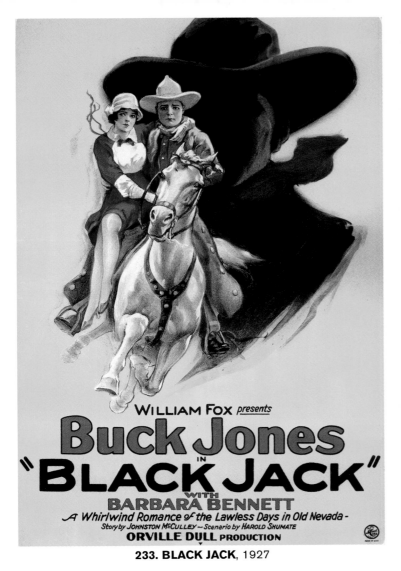

233. BLACK JACK, 1927

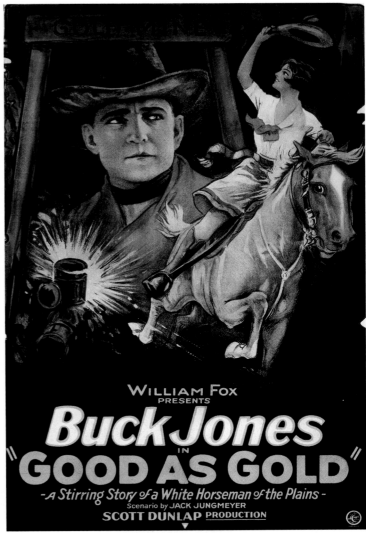

234. GOOD AS GOLD, 1927

235. MORGAN'S LAST RAID, 1929

236. CHAIN LIGHTNING, 1927

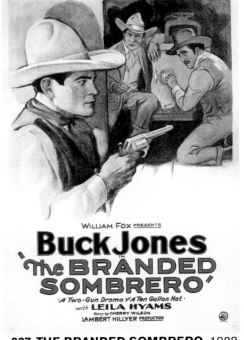

237. THE BRANDED SOMBRERO, 1928

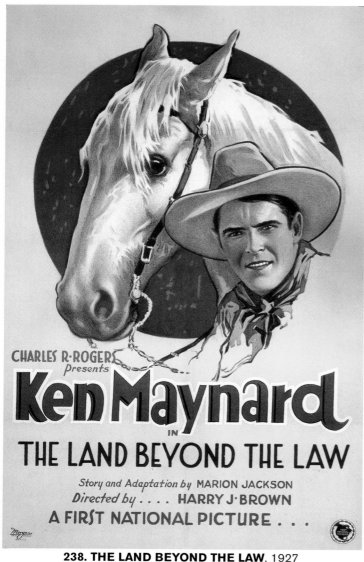

238. THE LAND BEYOND THE LAW, 1927

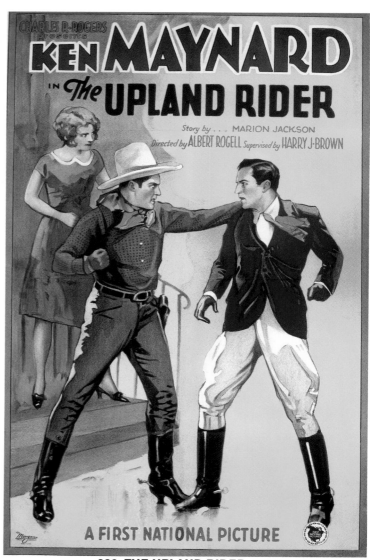

239. THE UPLAND RIDER, 1928

240. HEY! HEY! COWBOY, 1927

241. THE BUCKAROO KID, 1926

242. THE RAWHIDE KID, 1928

243. CUSTER'S LAST FIGHT, 1912, six-sheet, 1925 re-release (re-edited with new scenes, to commemorate the 50th anniversary of the Little Big Horn)

244. CUSTER'S LAST FIGHT, 1912, lobby cards, 1925 re-release

245. THE COWBOY KID, 1928

246. SILVER COMES THRU, 1927

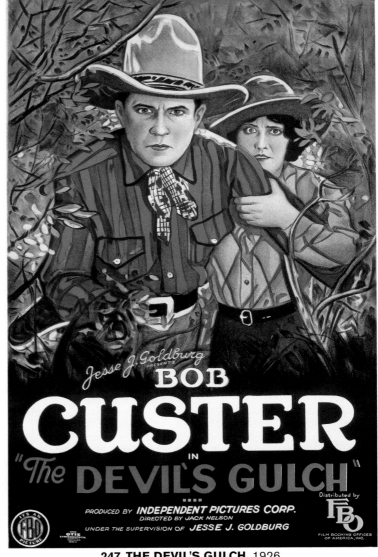

247. THE DEVIL'S GULCH, 1926

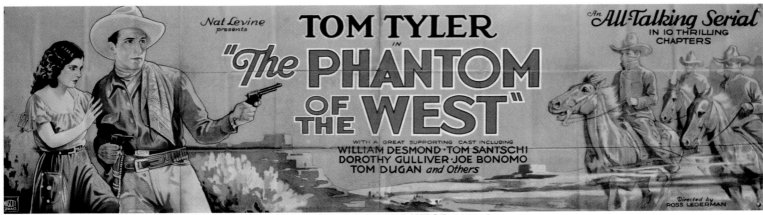

248. THE PHANTOM OF THE WEST, 1931, banner

249. THE VANISHING RIDER, 1928

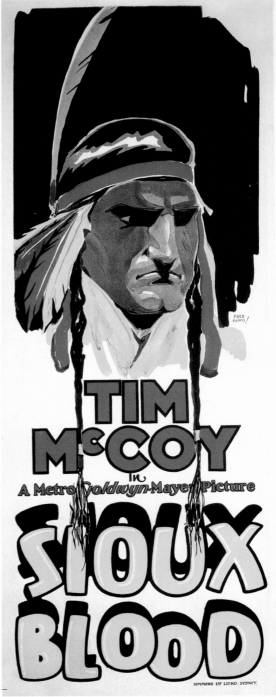

250. SIOUX BLOOD, 1929, Australian daybill

251. NO LOT

252. A FISTFUL OF DOLLARS, 1967

253. A FISTFUL OF DOLLARS, 1967, insert

254. A FISTFUL OF DOLLARS, 1964 first Italian poster, two-panel

255. A FISTFUL OF DOLLARS, 1965 Italian re-release, two-panel

256. FOR A FEW DOLLARS MORE, 1967, insert

257. THE GOOD, THE BAD AND THE UGLY, 1968, insert

258. DIRTY HARRY, 1971

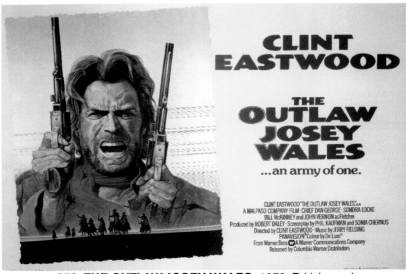

259. THE OUTLAW JOSEY WALES, 1976, British quad

260. BALL OF FIRE, 1941, autographed by Barbara Stanwyck

261. MEET JOHN DOE, 1941

262. MR BLANDINGS BUILDS HIS DREAM HOUSE, 1948, Australian daybill

263. BOOM TOWN, 1940, special one-sheet

264. GILDA, 1946, Italian lobby card

265. IT'S A WONDERFUL LIFE, 1946, autographed by James Stewart

266. COOL HAND LUKE, 1967, 4 door panels

267. THE HUSTLER, 1961, Italian locandina

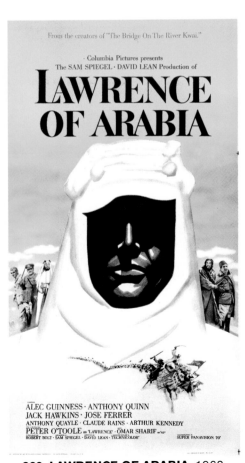

268. COOL HAND LUKE, 1967, lobby cards

269. LAWRENCE OF ARABIA, 1962, three-sheet

270. LAWRENCE OF ARABIA, 1962, French

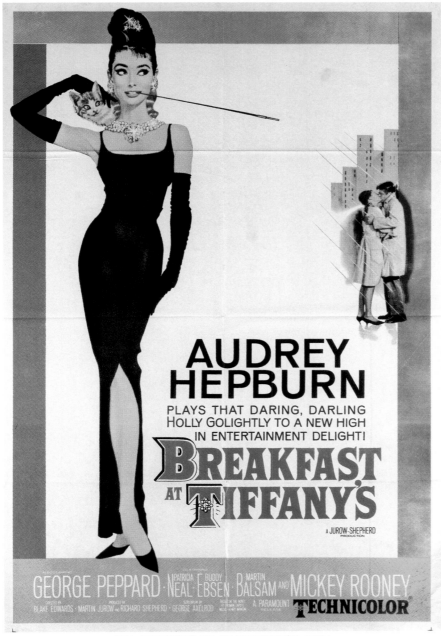

271. BREAKFAST AT TIFFANY'S, 1961

272. THE FBI STORY, 1959

273. A PLACE IN THE SUN,
1951, Australian one-sheet

274. BONJOUR TRISTESSE,
1958

275. NO WAY OUT,
1950, insert

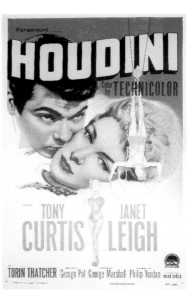

276. HOUDINI, 1953

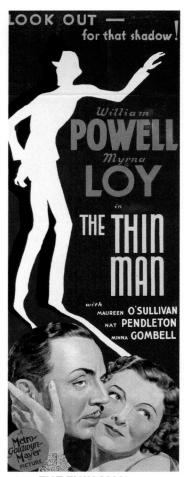

277. THE THIN MAN, 1934,
Australian daybill

**278. THE PRIVATE LIVES OF
ELIZABETH AND ESSEX**, 1939,
Australian daybill

279. GREAT GUY, 1936,
Australian daybill

280. COME AND GET IT, 1936,
insert

281. MARIE ANTOINETTE, 1938, French

282. YOU SAID A MOUTHFUL, 1932

283. MEN ARE NOT GODS, 1936

284. THE ADVENTURES OF ROBIN HOOD, 1938, English one-sheet, first English release (circa 1950)

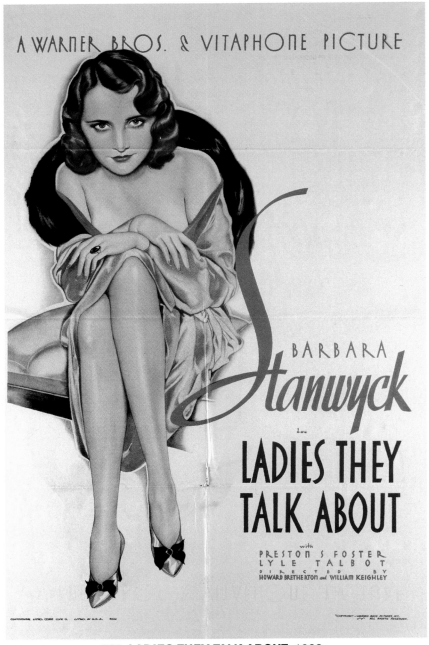

285. LADIES THEY TALK ABOUT, 1933

286. LADIES THEY TALK ABOUT, 1933, lobby cards

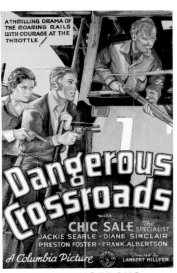

287. DANGEROUS CROSSROADS, 1933

288. I AM A FUGITIVE FROM A CHAIN GANG, 1932, Swedish

289. DANTE'S INFERNO, 1935

290. MR. SMITH GOES TO WASHINGTON, 1939, Belgian

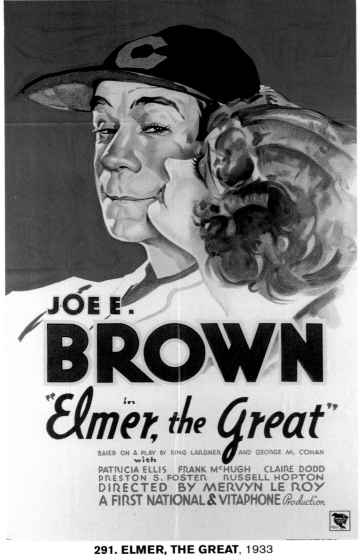

291. ELMER, THE GREAT, 1933

292. FIRE OVER ENGLAND, 1937

293. THE ADVENTURES OF JANE ARDEN, 1939

294. DANCING LADY, 1933, window card

295. FIRE OVER ENGLAND, 1937, lobby cards

296. THE BAD AND THE BEAUTIFUL, 1953, German

297. THE AFRICAN QUEEN, 1952, British Front of House lobby card

298. CASABLANCA, 1942, 1949 re-release lobby cards

299. SULLIVAN'S TRAVELS, 1941, lobby card

300. THE GRADUATE, 1968

301. THE GRADUATE, 1968, British quad

302. CAT ON A HOT TIN ROOF, 1958

303. SUDDENLY LAST SUMMER, 1960, autographed by Elizabeth Taylor

304. CLEOPATRA, 1964, Italian photobusta

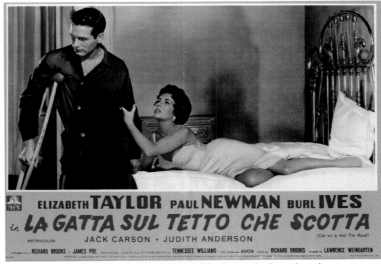

305. CAT ON A HOT TIN ROOF, 1958, Italian photobusta

306. THE STING, 1974

307. BUTCH CASSIDY AND THE SUNDANCE KID, 1969, half-sheet

308. BUTCH CASSIDY AND THE SUNDANCE KID, 1969

309. SHALL WE DANCE, 1937

310. FOOTLIGHT PARADE, 1933, window card

311. BRIGHT EYES, 1934, window card

312. STOWAWAY,
1936, Australian daybill

313. OUR LITTLE GIRL, 1935, window card

314. SINGIN' IN THE RAIN, 1952, autographed by Gene Kelly, Donald O'Connor, and Debbie Reynolds

315. THE GLENN MILLER STORY, 1954, German

316. THE BENNY GOODMAN STORY, 1956, German

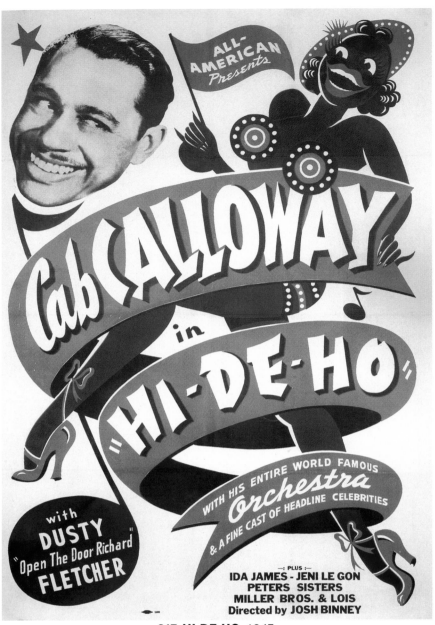

317. HI-DE-HO, 1947

318. WHITE CHRISTMAS, 1954

319. WHITE CHRISTMAS, 1954

320. LENA HORNE, 1940s, standee

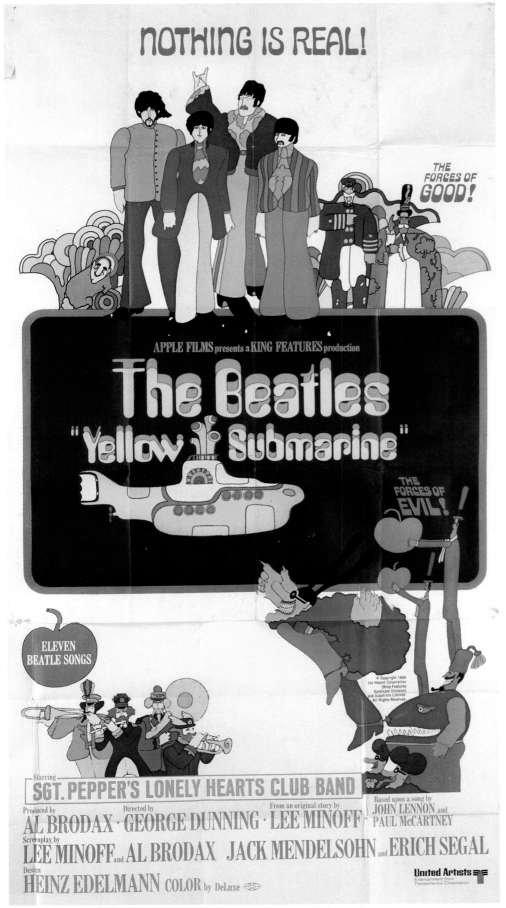

321. YELLOW SUBMARINE, 1968, three-sheet

322. A HARD DAY'S NIGHT, 1964

323. JIMI HENDRIX, 1973

324. JANIS, 1975

325. ON THE WATERFRONT, 1954, three-sheet

326. ON THE WATERFRONT, 1954, Italian

327. THE MEN, 1950, autographed by Marlon Brando

328. BULLITT, 1969

329. BULLITT, 1969, special poster

330. LE MANS, 1971, Japanese

331. THE GREAT ESCAPE, 1963

332. THE CINCINNATI KID, 1965, British quad

333. THE DEER HUNTER, 1978, English one-sheet

334. STAR WARS, 1977,
Thirty By Forty

**335. THE EMPIRE STRIKES
BACK**, 1980, Thirty By Forty

336. STAR TREK, 1979, German

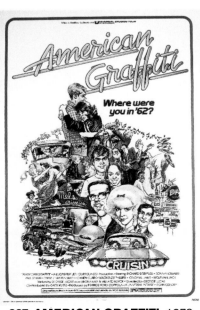

337. AMERICAN GRAFFITI, 1973

338. RETURN OF THE JEDI, 1983,
Thirty By Forty

339. DR. NO, 1962, British quad

340. DR. NO, 1962

341. DR. NO, 1962, Italian

342. FROM RUSSIA WITH LOVE, 1964, British quad

343. FROM RUSSIA WITH LOVE, 1964, half-sheet

344. FROM RUSSIA WITH LOVE, 1964

345. FROM RUSSIA WITH LOVE, 1964, French

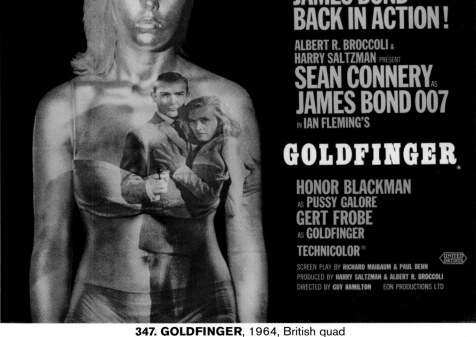

346. GOLDFINGER, 1964

347. GOLDFINGER, 1964, British quad

348. GOLDFINGER, 1964, French

349. THUNDERBALL, 1965, subway poster

350. THUNDERBALL, 1965, window card

351. THUNDERBALL, 1965, subway poster

352. THUNDERBALL, 1965, Italian

353. THUNDERBALL, 1965, subway poster

354. THUNDERBALL, 1965,
Thai c.1971

355. THUNDERBALL, 1965, half-sheet

356. THUNDERBALL,
1965, insert

**357. YOU ONLY LIVE
TWICE**, 1967, insert

358. YOU ONLY LIVE TWICE, 1967, subway poster

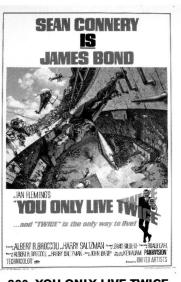

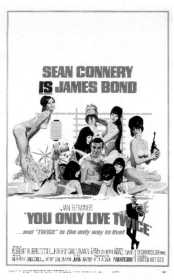

359. YOU ONLY LIVE TWICE,
1967

360. YOU ONLY LIVE TWICE,
1967

361. YOU ONLY LIVE TWICE,
1967, window card

362. YOU ONLY LIVE TWICE, 1967, half-sheet

363. ON HER MAJESTY'S SECRET SERVICE, 1970, half-sheet

365. DIAMONDS ARE FOREVER, 1971, British quad

364. DIAMONDS ARE FOREVER, 1971, six-sheet

366. DIAMONDS ARE FOREVER, 1971, half-sheet

367. THE MAN WITH THE GOLDEN GUN, 1974, British quad

368. THE MAN WITH THE GOLDEN GUN, 1974, Thirty By Forty

369. THE MAN WITH THE GOLDEN GUN, 1974

370. MOONRAKER, 1979, one-stop

IF YOU ENJOYED THIS MOVIE POSTER BOOK, THEN YOU ARE SURE TO ENJOY THESE OTHER SIMILAR BRUCE HERSHENSON PUBLICATIONS. LOOK FOR THEM AT YOUR LOCAL BOOKSTORE OR ORDER THEM DIRECT FROM THE PUBLISHER.

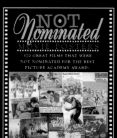

Vintage Hollywood Posters VI Index